# Content

The Earth's crust. 2
Under the Earth's crust. 4
How earthquakes happen. 6
A bad earthquake. 8
Earthquake in San Francisco. . . . 10
After an earthquake. 12
How volcanoes happen. 14
What is a volcano?. 16
A volcano erupts. 18
Mount Etna. 20
Sleeping volcanoes. 22
Index. 24

1

 # The Earth's crust

When you go for a walk, do you ever think about what is under your feet? You are walking on the Earth's crust. The Earth's crust is many kilometres deep.

Do you ever think about what is under your feet?

What is under the crust?

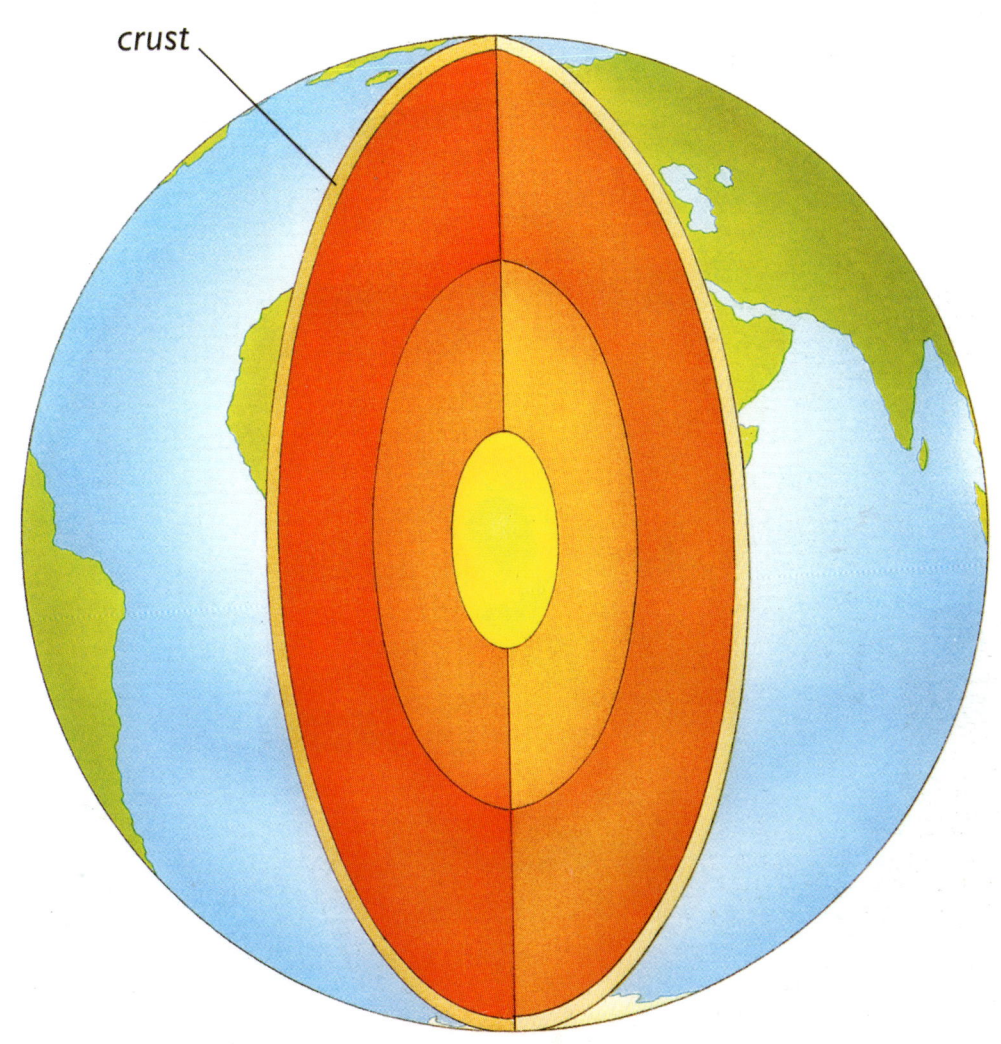

This is the planet Earth.

 # Under the Earth's crust

Under the Earth's crust is red hot rock.

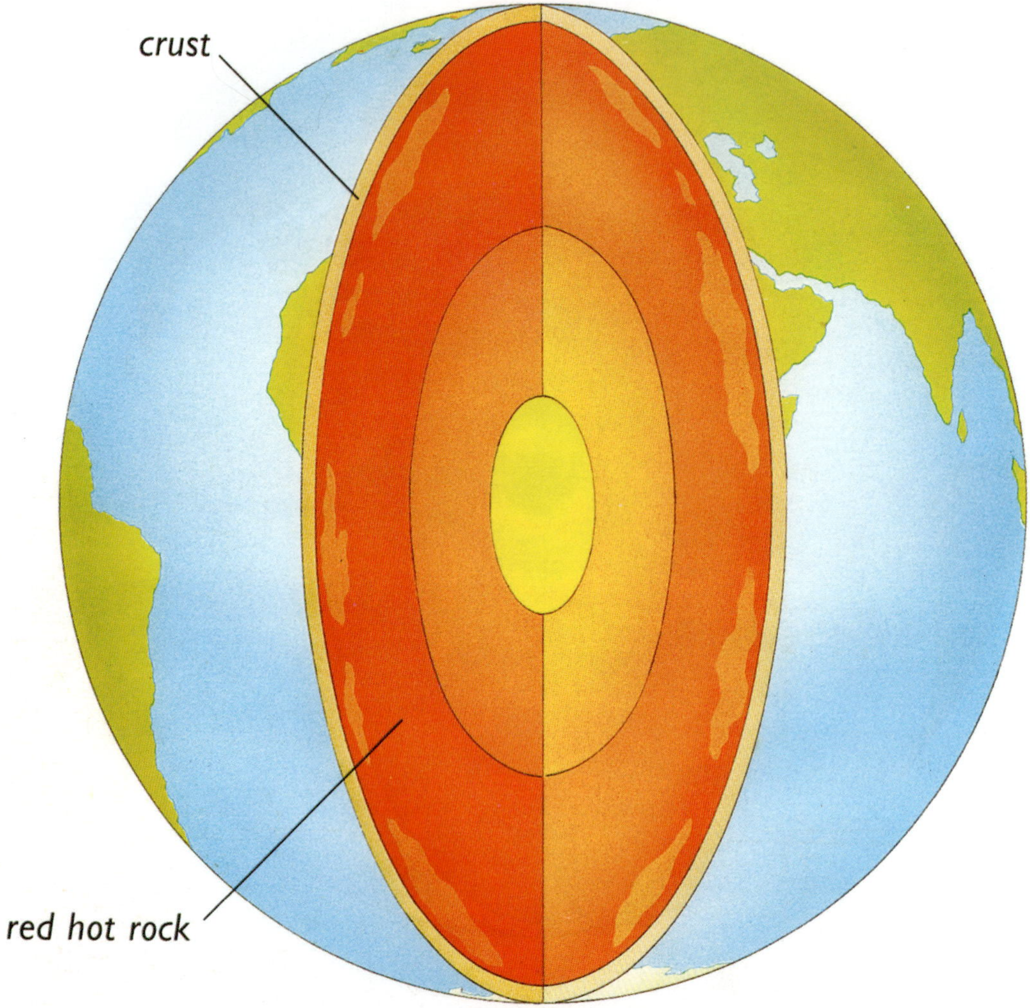

crust

red hot rock

Under the Earth's crust is red hot rock.

In some places the rock is so hot that it has melted. The Earth's crust sits on top of the red hot rock.

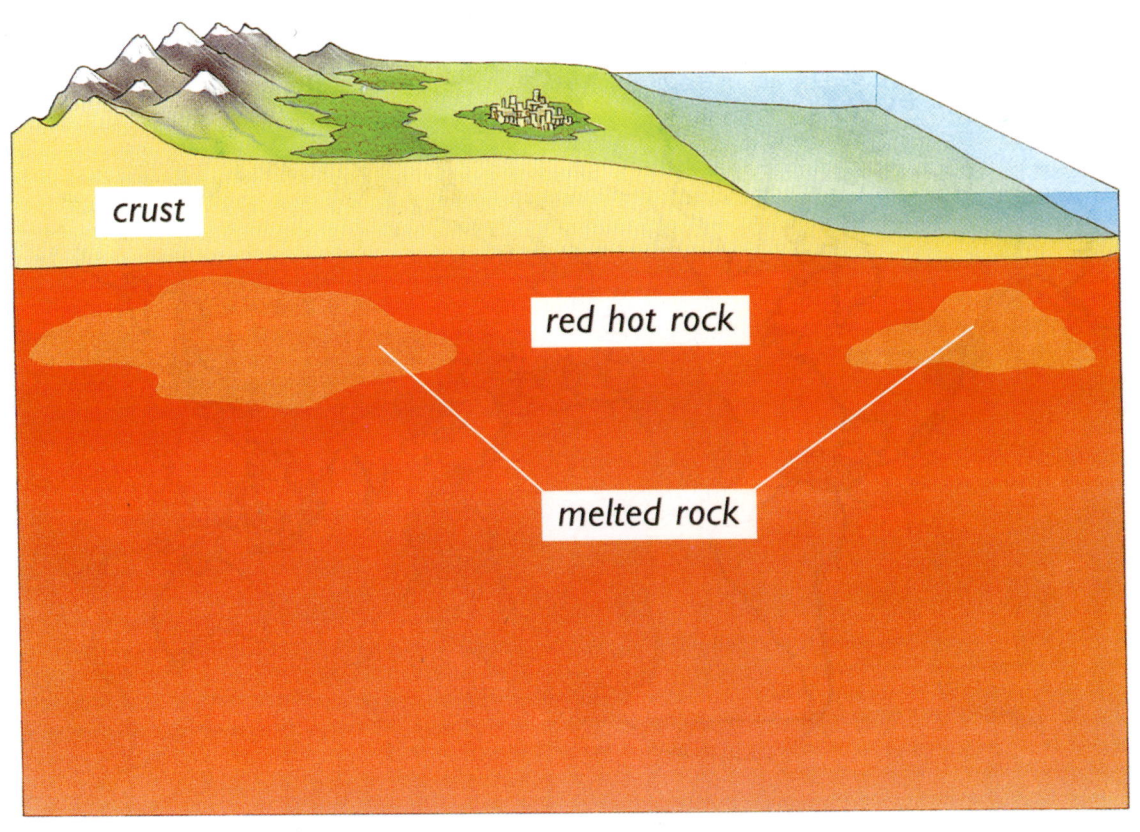

In some places the rock under the Earth's crust has melted.

How earthquakes happen

The Earth's crust is broken into pieces. It is a bit like a jigsaw puzzle, but with this jigsaw puzzle the pieces don't fit. Each piece moves slowly as it sits on the hot rock.

In this map of the world you can see where the crust is broken into pieces.

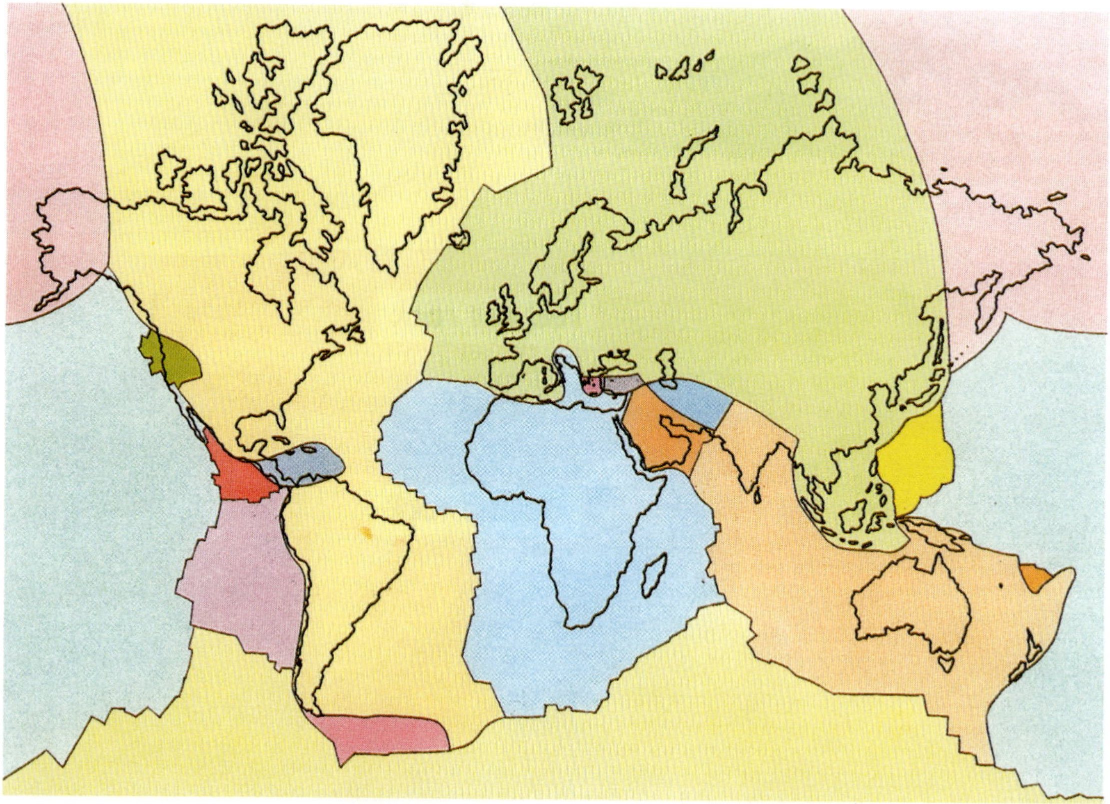

The Earth's crust is broken into pieces.

Sometimes some of the pieces of the Earth's crust push against each other. When this happens, the Earth's crust can crack. The ground above shakes. This is how an earthquake happens.

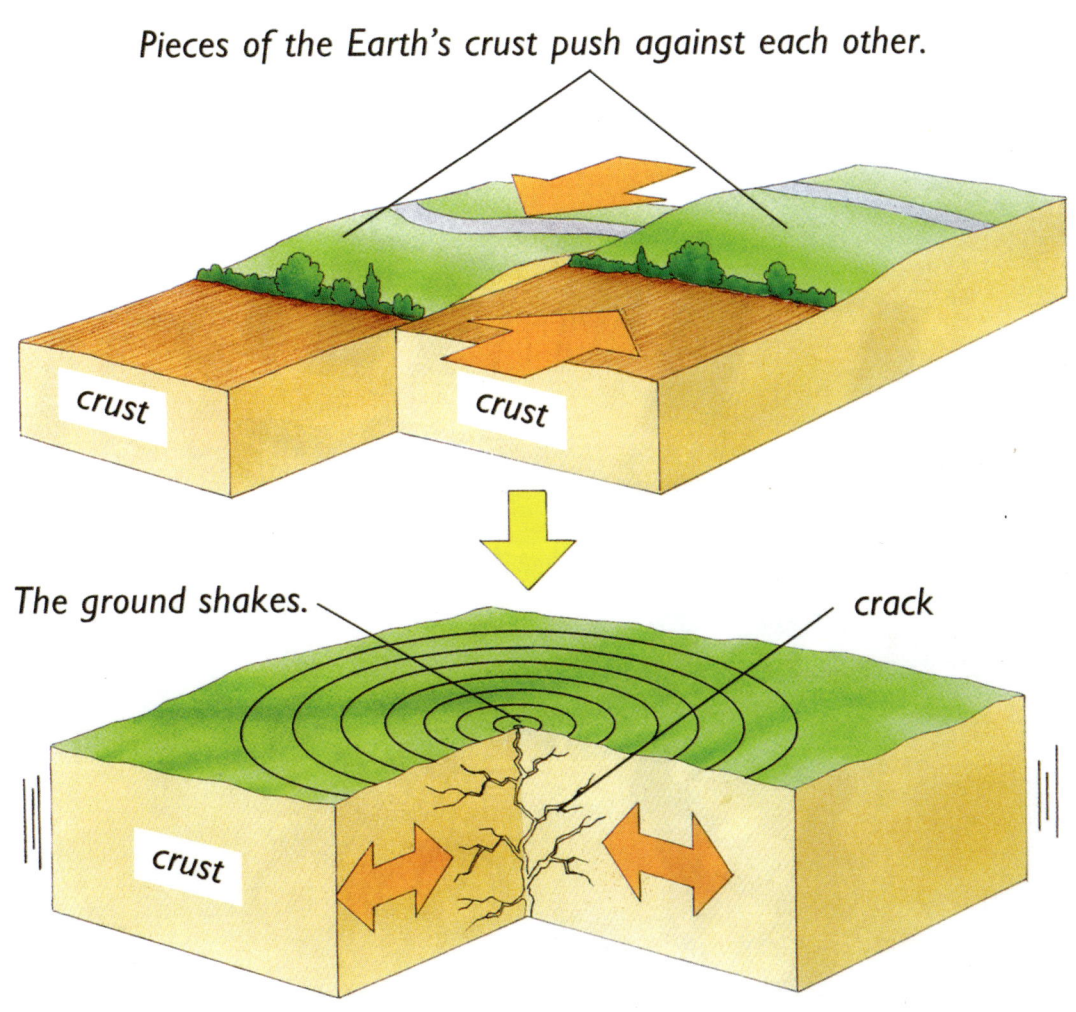

Pieces of the Earth's crust push against each other.

The ground shakes. crack

This is how an earthquake happens.

A bad earthquake

This is what happens during a bad earthquake. Houses fall down and roads split open.

This house fell down during a bad earthquake.

This road split open during a bad earthquake.

Earthquake in San Francisco

The town of San Francisco in America sits on a crack in the Earth's crust. People who live in San Francisco know that an earthquake can happen at any time.

In 1989, there was a bad earthquake in San Francisco. Some houses, roads and bridges fell down.

This road fell down during the 1989 San Francisco earthquake.

Many of the tall buildings in San Francisco have been made so that they won't fall down in an earthquake.

This tall building in San Francisco has been made so that it won't fall down in an earthquake.

After an earthquake

A bad earthquake can make rocks slide down a mountain. It can start a fire, too.

A bad earthquake can start a fire.

An earthquake under the sea makes large waves. The large waves are dangerous if they crash into the land.

Waves crash into the land after an earthquake under the sea.

How volcanoes happen

A volcano is a crack in the Earth's crust. Sometimes the melted rock is pushed up to the top of the crack. As the rock cools down, it gets very hard. It can build and build into a big volcano.

This volcano is about 3500 metres high.

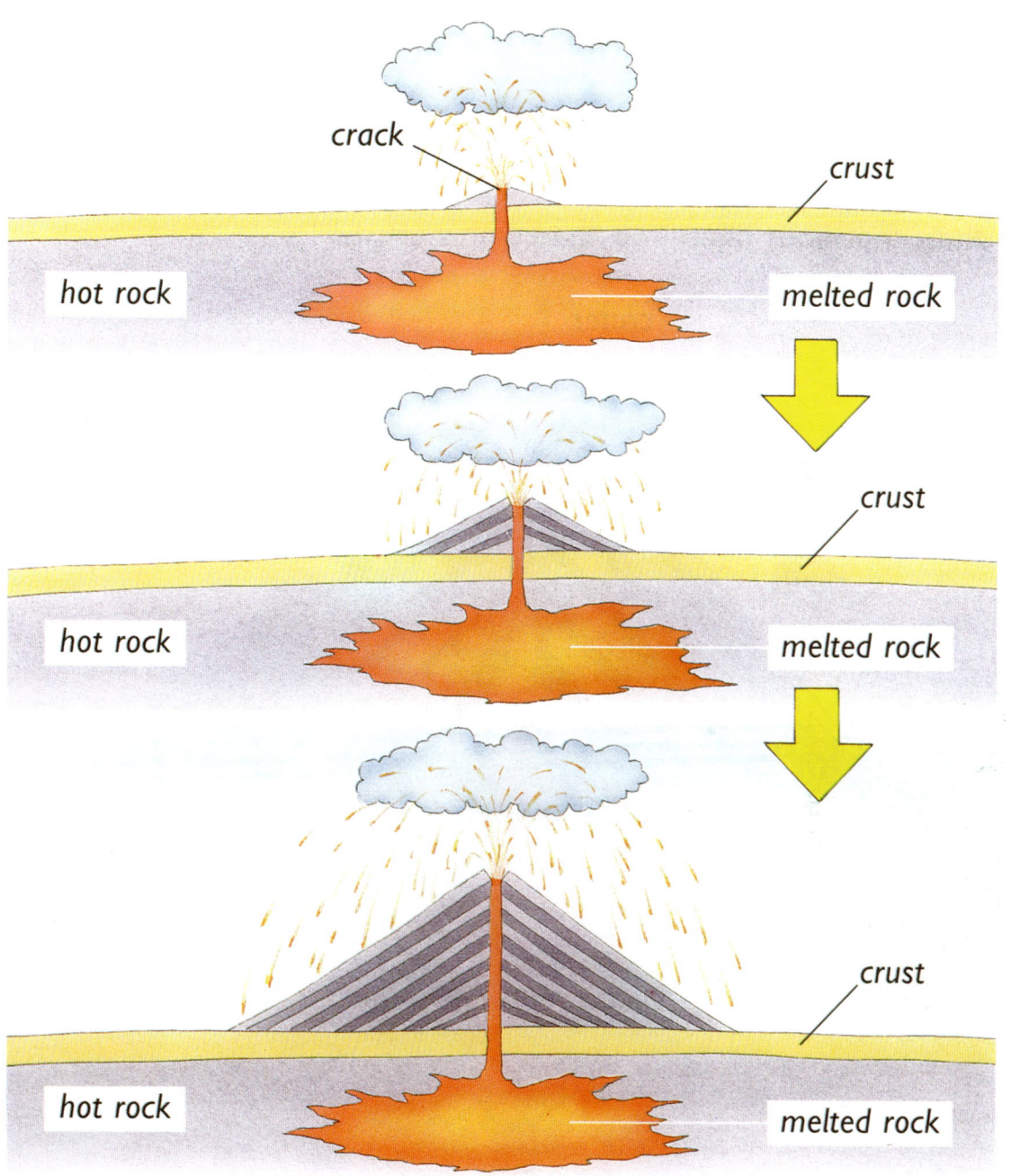

This is how a volcano happens.

15

What is a volcano?

This is a volcano. This volcano is like a hollow mountain. At the top of the volcano is a crater. The crater is at the top of a long shaft that goes deep into the Earth's crust.

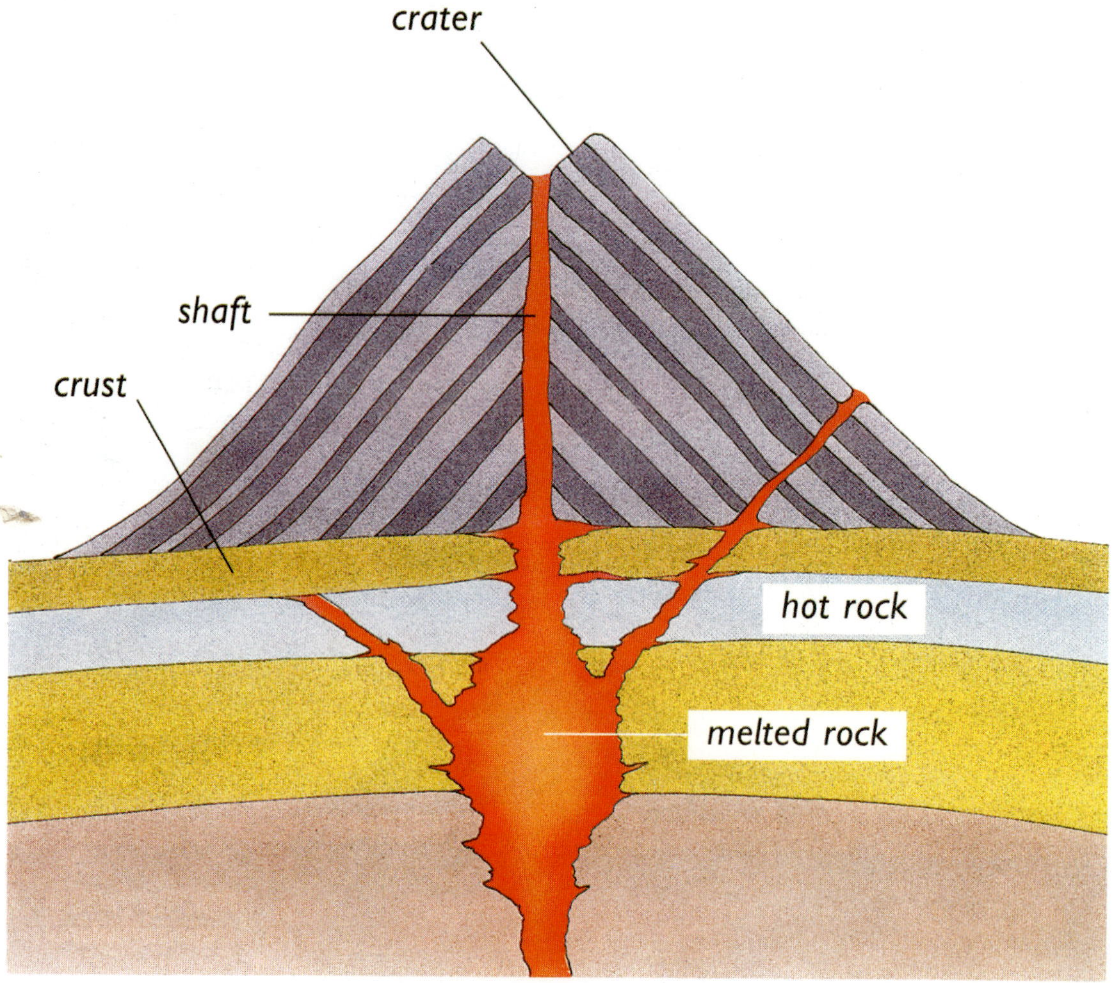

A volcano is like a hollow mountain.

Can you see the crater at the top of this volcano?

A volcano erupts

Sometimes a volcano erupts. When it erupts, ash, steam and melted rock shoot out of the crater. The melted rock is called lava.

A volcano starts to erupt.

Ash, steam and lava shoot out of the crater.

Mount Etna

This is a volcano called Mount Etna. Mount Etna is in Italy. It erupts every few years. The ash falls over the farmland. Then lava shoots out and creeps slowly over the land.

This is Mount Etna.

The lava cools and gets very hard.

This is the ash and lava on Mount Etna.

Sleeping volcanoes

Mount Etna is an active volcano. An active volcano erupts a lot.

Mount Etna erupts a lot.

22

Some volcanoes have not erupted for many, many years. These volcanoes are called sleeping volcanoes. Sleeping volcanoes are very dangerous because no one knows when they will erupt.

This is a sleeping volcano.

 # Index

A

ash............ 18, 20

C

crack.......... 7, 10, 14
crater........... 16, 18
crust........... 2, 3, 4,
　　　　5, 6, 7, 10, 14, 16

E

earthquake......... 7, 8,
　　　　10, 11, 12, 13

L

lava.......... 18, 20, 21

M

Mount Etna....... 20, 22
mountain......... 12, 16

R

rock....... 4, 5, 6, 14, 18

V

volcano.......... 14, 16,
　　　　18, 20, 22, 23